SUMMARY

Ibram X. Kendi's

HOW TO BE AN

ANTIRACIST

Table of contents

Introduction

In *How to Be an Antiracist,* **Ibram X. Kendi** discusses the different types of racism comprehensively at all levels of existence. He introduces us to the concept of antiracism in detail, so that we can start accepting the racist inside us all and work to become an antiracist instead of claiming that we are 'not racist.' He makes it easy for readers to notice and label racism in all its faces and see how it proves detrimental to society. He teaches us to begin with ourselves and then work to transform various systems to make our world antiracist.

Author's Introduction to Racism

The author, **Ibram X. Kendi**, who is a preacher's son, grew up seeing suit and tie wearing church people around him. He could not help detesting suits and ties. On the 17th of January, 2000, more than three thousand black people and a small number of white people came together at the Hylton Memorial Chapel in Northern Virginia. Kendi's parents were still surprised that he had reached the final stage of the Prince William County Martin Luther King Jr. debate contest. Even though most of Kendi's opponents wore a dark suit and tie with a white collar, Kendi opted for a golden-brown blazer, black shirt and a bright tie. Kendi's opponents were academic geniuses while he had a low GPA and SAT score.

Some weeks prior to this, Kendi was embarrassed by his father when he was on the basketball court with his high school team. His father made an emotional appearance to announce Kendi's surprise acceptance from Hampton University in Southern Virginia, not caring about white onlookers. His father never cared about judgment from white people. Kendi shared his tears of happiness with his father on hearing this news despite the judging white eyes surrounding them. He later ended up joining Florida A&M University, the only other college he had applied to. He only applied to two universities because he considered himself to be stupid. He thought he was not a good student and this idea stemmed from the messages he received from the media

Internalized Racism

At the afore-mentioned event, Kendi gave an emotional speech. He is ashamed of the speech he gave at the contest even today. He highlighted the things wrong with black youth by referring to the latter as 'they'. He stated all the racist things that society made him think were true about black youth even though they were not. His speech was a result of internalized racism. On MLK Day 2000, he believed that black people themselves were the problem.

Living in Denial

Today, Donald Trump criticizes people from other races endlessly. He declared black people to be characteristically lazy a long time ago. He promoted the idea of building a wall because he blamed

Latin American people for being rapists and criminals. He promoted a Muslim ban. He called his black critics foolish. Donald Trump's blatant racism does not stop here. He keeps repeating things like this. What makes matters worse is that he claims to be the least racist person around. This denial is not uncommon amongst racists. They never accept that they are racist.

The Claim of being 'Not Racist'

Denial is at the core of racism and common across countries, races and ideologies. Even several of us who realize the racism in Trump would not be able to acknowledge our own. We become defensive when someone calls anything we say or think defensive. Trump and several white supremacists think they are 'not racist.' We also have our own way of defining that we are 'not racist.'

The Difference between 'Not Racist' and 'Antiracist'

The issue with being 'not racist' is that it makes a claim about being neutral. People who declare that they are 'not racist' might not be passionately against racism. It is a huge issue because the fight against racism does not benefit from neutrality. The contradiction of 'racist' is never 'not racist.' It is actually 'antiracist.'

The difference between the two terms is clear. A person can either think as a racist and believe in the notion of a racial ladder or think like an antiracist and believe in 'racial equality.' A person can further believe like a racist that problems originate from groups of people or think like an antiracist that problems stem from policies and power. An individual either lets racial inequities persist as a racist or challenges racial inequities as an antiracist. The comfortably middle area of 'not racist' does not exist. The declaration of 'not racist' impartiality is often utilized to conceal racism. Even though this might seem too strict, it is among the most fundamental principles of antiracism to send the word 'racist' back to its suitable usage.

Racist is not equal to a slur. The word is descriptive and we can only cancel racism by regularly recognizing and describing it. The next step is to rip it to shreds. If we try to transform the expressive term of racist into an unworkable slur, it will stop us from taking any action.

Color Blindness

Some people also declare themselves to be color blind. It is also an equivalent of being 'not racist.' A color blind person who does not notice race is also unable to notice racism and falls victim to racist passivity. Color blindness, just like being 'not racist' is a veil to conceal racism.

Racist and Antiracist Ideas

Racist and antiracist do not fall under the label of static identities. We might act like a racist right now but like an antiracist the next second. Our momentary actions and words define 'what' we are in a particular moment. Kendi believes that he identified with racists earlier by calling himself 'not racist.' However, he has now become an antiracist. He does not believe anymore that a Black person cannot be racist. He does not try to persuade White people of his equal humanity. He does not worry anymore about what the actions of other Black people say about him. He does not try to persuade Black people that he is symbolizing the race well, and so on.

This book covers the fundamental battle we are going through, to be completely human and understand that others are completely human too. We know the way to be racist. We know the way to fake being 'not racist.' Let us learn the way to be an antiracist.

Chapter 1: Definitions

Racist

A racist is someone who supports a racist policy through voicing a racist idea or his actions or inaction.

Antiracist

An antiracist is someone who supports a racist policy through stating an antiracist idea or through his actions.

Kendi's Parents and the Definition of Christianity

Kendi's parents separately reached the same conclusion about Christianity. His father, Larry, learned from James Cone, the academic father of Black liberation theology, that a Christian struggles to achieve liberation. His mother, Carol, also learned that Christianity entails struggle and liberation. This notion changed and defined their lives from then on.

Kendi's Journey as an Antiracist

Kendi's journey as an antiracist began in 1970 right there because his parents' direction of change transformed the lives of their then future sons forever. This new definition of Christian existence provided the foundation for Larry and Carol's lives and their children's lives to come. Kendi cannot untangle his parents' religious attempts to be Christian from his secular endeavors to be antiracist. The most significant step for both of them was to define their terms so that they would be able to start describing the world and their position in it. Definitions help us stay rooted in principles. If we fail to carry out the fundamental task of defining the type of people we wish to be in words that are balanced and steady, then we will be unable to work to achieve balanced and reliable goals.

How to Be an Antiracist

To be an antiracist equals coming up with coherent definitions of racism /antiracism, racist /antiracist notions, racist/antiracist policies, and racist /antiracist people.

How to Be a Racist

To be a racist equals redefining racist endlessly in such a manner that it will absolve a person's transforming notions, policies and personhood.

Definition of Racism

Racism refers to the mixing of racist ideas and racist policies that generates and regularizes racial imbalances.

Racial Inequity

Racial inequity means two or more racial groups not standing on an almost similar basis.

Racist Policy

A racist policy refers to any measure that generates or supports racial inequity between racial groups.

12

Antiracist Policy

An antiracist policy refers to any measure that generates or supports racial equity between racial groups.

Policy in this context means both written and unwritten rules, laws, processes, procedures, guidelines and regulations that administrate people. Nonracist or race-neutral policy does not exist. Each policy is either racist or antiracist. Other terms that have been used to describe racist policy include systematic racism, "structural racism" and institutional racism.

Racial Discrimination

Racial discrimination refers to an instantaneous and noticeable demonstration of a primary racial policy. The sole cure for racist discrimination is antiracist discrimination.

Racist Idea

A racist idea refers to any idea that proposes that one racial group is better or worse than another racial group in any manner. Racist ideas maintain that merits and demerits of racial groups clarify racial inequities.

Antiracist Idea

An antiracist idea means any idea that advises that the racial groups are equals in every outward difference and that nothing is right or wrong with any racial group. Antiracist ideas claim that racist policies give birth to racial inequities.

Comprehending the differences between these definitions permits us to go back to our basic definitions.

Racism

Racism refers to a potent assortment of racist policies that cause racial inequity and are validated by racist ideas.

Antiracism

Antiracism means a potent assembly of antiracist policies that give rise to racial equity and are endorsed by antiracist ideas.

Firm definitions of racism and antiracism can help us begin to comprehend the racialized environment around us.

Chapter 2: Dueling Consciousness

Assimilationist

This term refers to a person who demonstrates the racist idea that a racial group is substandard in its culture or behavior and supports cultural or behavioral improvement plans to advance that racial group.

Segregationist

This term means a person that demonstrates the racist idea that it is impossible to develop a lastingly second-rate racial group and favors policy that isolates that racial group.

Antiracist

Antiracist means someone who demonstrates the idea that racial groups are equals and there is no need to develop any of them. Such a person also favors policy that lessens racial inequity.

Dueling Consciousness

What has contributed to the environment of racism in America is that Americans have been prepared to observe the shortcomings of people instead of policy. Both white and black people have dueling consciousness. White people have their own version of dueling consciousness between the assimilationist and the segregationist. Assimilationist ideas and segregationist ideas fall under the category of racist ideas, the duel within racist thought. White assimilationist ideas defy segregationist ideas that argue that people of color lack the ability to develop, attain higher standards, and be White and therefore do not have the capability to be completely human. On the contrary, assimilationists think that people of color can be developed and be completely human, like White people. Assimilationist ideas bring down people of color to the level of children requiring instructions on how they should act. Segregationist ideas completely isolate people of color as 'animals', considering them to be devoid of the ability to be taught.

17

The Three-Way Battle

The racialized world has been going through a fight between segregationists, assimilationists and antiracists. Antiracist ideas stem from the truth that racial groups are equals in every single way that they are different. Assimilationist ideas stem from the view that specific racial groups are behaviorally or culturally substandard. Segregationist ideas originate from having faith in genetic racial division and fixed hierarchy.

David Hume professed that every race is created unequal but Thomas Jefferson apparently differed in 1776 when he avowed that "all men are created equal." However, Thomas Jefferson did not make the antiracist announcement. He never said all racial groups are equals. On the one hand, segregationist ideas consider a racial group to be eternally inferior. On the other hand, assimilationist ideas propose that a racial group is momentarily substandard.

The dueling White consciousness gave rise to two categories of racist policies, shedding light on the battle between racist ideas. Assimilationists theorize behavioral and cultural order.

Assimilationist programs and policies aim to grow, refine and integrate a racial group (different from programs that elevate individuals). Segregationist policies aim to cut off, enslave, imprison, deport and execute people of color. Antiracists suggest that racial groups are civilized already and such policies aim to lessen racial inequities and introduce equal chances.

White people have tried to introduce both assimilationist and segregationist policies in general. People of color have tried to introduce both antiracist and assimilationist policies.

The Struggle within Black Consciousness

Since the dueling White consciousness has enjoyed a status of comparative power, therefore, it has molded the struggle within black consciousness. Black consciousness operates from a position where it considers Whites to be superior and tries to reach that position.

The White body is the definition of the American body. The White body isolates the Black body from the American body. The White body directs the Black body to assimilate into the American body, and consciousness and history battle once again. The Black body goes through the same battle. The Black body is directed to be an American body. The American body is another name for the White body. The Black body attempts to assimilate into the American body. The American body rejects the Black body. The Black body detaches from the American body. The cycle continues. Consciousness and history keep battling.

Chapter 3: Power

Race

Race is a power paradigm of gathered or combined difference that dwells socially.

Racism has the power to take over people. Race is a dominant construction that can devour us. However, despite that life-shaping power, race is a kind of mirage, which does not reduce its force. We are what we consider ourselves to be, regardless of whether it is correct or not. We are also what other people consider us to be, whether it is true or not. What people notice in themselves and others has meaning and exhibits itself in ideas, actions and policies, despite the possibility of what they are seeing as an illusion. Race is a fantasy but the kind that we do well to notice, while not letting it out of our mind that it is a mirage, not letting it out of mind that the powerful light of racist power contributes to the mirage.

An irony of antiracism requires us to identify racially so that we can recognize the racial privileges and hazards of existing in our bodies.

Chapter 4: Biology

Biological Racist

It refers to a person who demonstrates the idea that the races are profoundly different when it comes to biology and these differences give birth to a hierarchy of value.

Biological Antiracist

It refers to a person who is demonstrating the idea that the races are importantly similar in their biology and there are no racial differences at the genetic level.

Microaggression

The term was coined to refer to the continual verbal and nonverbal abuse racist White people subject Black people to, regardless of where they are. Microaggression is different from macroaggression, which refers to racial violence and policies.

Biological differences, such as different skin colors, do not matter to our principal humanity, which is the crux of biological antiracism. A lot of people think and act like these shallow variances imply different types of humanity, which is the core of biological racism.

Biological racists are segregationists. Some segregationists believe that if humans are 99.9% similar genetically, then they should be 0.1% unique. And this uniqueness must be racial. And this 0.1% of racial division has multiplied exponentially over time. And it is their responsibility to look for the proper place for these exponentially distinctive races.

Assimilationists have taken another responsibility, and it has been in the making for decades. They trust the post-racial myth that discussing race creates racism or that if we do not classify by race, racism will just disappear magically. They do not comprehend that if we avoid utilizing racial categories, then we will fail to recognize racial inequity. If we fail to recognize racial inequity, then we will not be able to recognize racist policies. If we cannot recognize racist policies, then we will not be able to challenge racist policies. If we fail to challenge racist policies, then we will reach the final solution of racist power, i. e. a realm of inequity no one can see. When we cannot even see it, we will not be able to fight it. Eliminating racial classifications might be the last, instead of the first, step in the antiracist battle.

Segregationists consider six biologically unique races. Assimilationists notice a single biological human race. Biological antiracism is another manner of considering this. It means to be aware of the truth about biological equality, that skin color is as useless as our clothes in the context of our core humanity.

Chapter 5: Ethnicity

Ethnic Racism

The term refers to a powerful assortment of racist policies that create inequity between racialized ethnic groups and are validated by racist ideas about racialized ethnic groups.

Ethnic Antiracism

This term refers to a powerful array of antiracist policies that give birth to equity between racialized ethnic groups and are authenticated by antiracist ideas about racialized ethnic groups.

The roots of ethnic racism could be traced back to the slave trade's supply-and-demand market for people products. Different enslavers had different preferences concerning distinct ethnic groups in Africa, thinking some of them made better slaves. White people have been subjecting African Americans to racism for a long time. However, Blacks also subject other racial groups to racism at times.

Africans Americans have racist ideas about Africans, West Indians and others. They consider immigrants from Africa and South America inferior. White people have racist ideas about a lot of ethnic groups including African Americans, Latin Americans, Asians, etc.

Ethnically racist ideas, like other racist ideas, conceal the racist policies exercised against Black natives and immigrants. When Black immigrants weigh their economic status against that of Black natives, when they agree that their success demonstrates that antiracist Americans are exaggerating racist policies against African Americans, they are constricting the shackles of racist policy around themselves. Comparison of Black immigrants with Black natives hides the racial inequities between Black immigrants and non-Black immigrants.

Studies demonstrate that Black immigrants are the most literate group of immigrants in the United States on average. However, they have less income than identically trained non-Black immigrants and the biggest unemployment rate of any immigrant group.

Chapter 6: Body

Bodily Racist

It refers to a person who considers specific racialized bodies as more like animals and violent than others.

Bodily Antiracist

It refers to a person who civilizes, deracializes and individualizes violent and nonviolent behavior.

History lets us know that violence for White people has had a Black face for a long time and the Black body has suffered because of it. White Americans started considering African Americans to be 'wild beasts' who can consume anyone. The existing legacy of racist power is to build the Black race biologically and ethnically and exhibit the Black body to the world as a monster, as cruelly dangerous, as a dark personification of evil. Research indicates that today's Americans view the Black body as bigger, more possibly detrimental, more intimidating and more likely to need force to regulate than an identically sized White body.

This perception persists despite the fact that researchers have discovered a more powerful and obvious correlation between violent crime levels and unemployment levels than between violent crime and race.

Chapter 7: Culture

Cultural Racist

It refers to a person who develops a cultural standard and enforces a cultural hierarchy among racial groups.

Cultural Antiracist

It refers to a person who rejects cultural standards and evens out cultural differences among racist groups.

Segregationists believe that racial groups cannot grasp their higher cultural standard. Assimilationists believe that racial groups can reach their higher cultural standards with purpose and hard work. The key point of all of this is that White Americans believe African Americans to be the backward race with an inferior culture.

When we call a group White or Black or some other racial identity, we end up racializing that group. When we racialize a group and then term its culture substandard, we are expressing cultural racism.

To be an antiracist means to consider all cultures in their differences to be on an identical level. We should consider cultural differences to be cultural differences, nothing more than that.

Chapter 8: Behavior

Behavioral Racist

Such a racist considers individuals to be responsible for the supposed behavior of racial groups and racial groups to be responsible for the behavior of individuals.

Behavioral Antiracist

Such a person considers racial group behavior to be imaginary and individual behavior to be real.

Behavioral racism contaminates our opinion of the world in two ways i. e. considering individuals to be responsible for the supposed behavior of racial groups and considering entire racial groups to be responsible for the behavior of individuals. When we think that a racial group's apparent success or failure comes back to a whole group, we have embraced a racist idea.

Excluding Black Minds and Bodies

The utilization of standardized tests to measure intelligence and skill is among the most effective racist policies ever devised to insult Black minds and reject Black bodies. We insult Black minds each time we discuss an academic achievement gap rooted in these numbers.

How to Test People Correctly

A significant number of initiatives have tried to reduce the achievement gap. However, they might have been a way to let racist ideas in. We have to consider if different environments give rise to unique types of achievement instead of unique levels of achievement. The intellect of a Black child in a poor Black school, who tests low on a test, might just be different from but not less than that of a White child in a wealthy White school, who tests high. We need to consider the possibility of measuring intelligence by the degree of knowledge of individuals about their own surroundings and by their aspiration to learn. We need to ponder what would happen if we tried to make our educational system effective not by standardizing our syllabi and examinations but by standardizing the prospects students can have.

Racism vs. Antiracism

If we keep thinking that something is wrong with the behavior of a racial group, our mind cannot be antiracist. If our mind keeps repressing the oppressed by believing that their oppressive environment has stunted their behavior, our mind will never be able to be antiracist.

To be an antiracist means believing that behaviorally, nothing is right or wrong, superior or inferior, with any racial group. When the antiracist notices individuals acting positively or negatively, the antiracist notices only that, instead of symbols of entire races. To be antiracist means deracializing behavior, eliminating the engraved stereotype from each racialized body. It means to believe that behavior is something done by humans instead of races.

Chapter 9: Color

Colorism

It refers to a powerful assembly of racist policies that create inequities between light- and dark-skinned people, strengthened by racist ideas about both sorts of people.

Color Antiracism

It refers to a powerful pool of antiracist policies that give rise to equity between dark and light people, strengthened by antiracist ideas about dark and light people.

The dueling consciousness consisting of antiracist pride in a person's own race and assimilationist longing to be part of another race leads to the absurd post-racial beauty ideal. It keeps multiculturalism, inclusion and freshness working in parallel with Eurocentricism, exclusion and outdated ways.

The post-racial beauty ideal conceals colorism and covers it with understatement. Colorism is another face of racism. To identify colorism, we first need to identify that Dark people and Light people are two different racial groups molded by their specific histories. Dark people, the undisclosed racial group of darker skins, twisty hair, and wider lips and noses are discovered in several nationalities, ethnicities and races.

Light people often fall into the White category and might be acknowledged into Whiteness so that White people can sustain majorities in countries such as the United States, where demographic inclinations threaten to demote them to minority status. Some reformers portray Light people as the biracial key to racial coherence, a personification of a "post-racial future."

Colorism is a group of racist policies that lead to inequities between Dark people and Light people. These inequities are validated by racist ideas about Dark people and Light people. Colorism follows the examples of other types of racism by justifying inequities with racist ideas. It asserts that inequities between Dark people and Light people stem from what is right or wrong with these groups of people instead of racist policy. Colorist ideas are similar to assimilationist ideas in the sense that they endorse assimilation or conversion into something like the White body.

An antiracist concentrates on color lines equally as racial lines, being aware that color lines have the potential to be as damaging as racial lines for Dark people. Dark people time and again do not notice colorism despite experiencing it consistently since discriminations between the races outshine inequities within the races.

Anti-Dark racism adheres to the logic of behavioral racism, connecting behavior to color. White children characterize positivity to lighter skin and negativity to darker. This colorism strengthens as they grow up. White people mostly favor light-skinned politicians over dark-skinned ones. Dark African-American students have considerably lower GPAs than Light students. It might be because of higher expectations from Light students. Employers have a fondness for Light Black men over Dark Black men, irrespective of their qualifications. Light daughters and Dark sons receive better parenting. Lighter Black women are considered to be better-looking and their self-esteem is also higher. Dark African Americans receive the toughest prison sentences and more time in prison. Inequities between Dark and Light African Americans could be as evident as those between White and Black Americans.

Some Dark people are excessively proud of being dark and might question the Blackness of lighter skinned people.

Chapter 10: White

Anti-White Racist

Such a racist considers people of European descent to be biologically, culturally or behaviorally substandard or associates the whole race of White people with racist power. Black people can also be racist toward White people. Malcolm X, who had been a torch-bearer for the Nation of Islam before his conversion to orthodox Islam, understood it. An example of Black people's racism against White people is the White-devil idea propagated by Nation of Islam.

White people that welcome racist ideas and policies and then deny doing so are wrong. But there is no such thing as White genes. We should only raise a voice against problematic trends. We need to untangle the greedy, prejudiced, aggressive and individualist cultures of racial capitalism and modern empire from the cultures of White people. They are not identical.

An antiracist does not confuse the worldwide march for White racism for the worldwide march for White people. An antiracist does not complicate the antiracist hate for White racism by adding racist hate for White people to it. To be antiracist equals not combine racist people with White people, knowing that antiracist Whites and racist non-Whites exist.

Chapter 11: White

Powerless Defense

This term refers to the racist, masking, disempowering and deceptive idea that Black people cannot be racist because they have no power. A number of Black people refer to a group of other Black people as niggers. They separate themselves from the term nigger. Comedian Chris Rock made the racial construct of 'them niggers' famous in his 1996 HBO special, *Bring the Pain*. He then spoke about Black people and their "personal civil war." He said that he loved Black people but he hated niggers. This is part of the dueling consciousness in a huge number of Black people. Chris Rock assisted Black people in reconstructing the racial group as 'niggers' and allocating qualities to this group. Niggers are considered to impede Black people having a good time. They are quite loud. They are talking all the time, asking for credit for looking after their children and saving themselves from prison. Chris Rock added that niggers hate books because they just love being ignorant. He refuted the antiracist assertion that the media had twisted the image of Blacks to make them seem bad. He blamed it on the niggers.

Chris Rock underlined that the Black man and the nigger are two separate entities. It was a remix of the idea that the White man and the Negro are unequal. What happened there was that Black people did not categorize loud folks who were Black as an interracial group of loud people-as antiracists. Black people racialized the undesirable behavior and attributed loudness to niggers, following the example of White racists, as Black racists. In this case, Black people did not categorize negligent Black parents under an interracial group of negligent parents-as antiracists. They racialized the undesirable behavior and attributed negligent parenting to niggers, shadowing White racists, as Black racists. They did not classify Black criminals into an interracial group of criminals-as antiracists. They racialized the negative behavior and attributed delinquency to niggers, following White racists, as Black racists. They further did not position lazy Blacks into an interracial group of lazy people —as antiracists. Here, Black people racialized the destructive behavior and ascribed laziness to niggers, resembling White racists, in the role of Black racists. In addition, post these developments, Black people self-acknowledged as 'not-racist', same as White racists, as Black racists.

Kendi thought only Whites could harbor racism and Blacks, Asians, Natives, Middle Easterners and Latinx could not, since the latter did not have any power. However, this "powerless defense" exists. It arose in the aftermath of racist Whites dismissing antiracist ideas and policies as racist in the late 1960s. In the decades that followed, Blacks protesting against White racism shielded themselves from these charges by claiming that Black people cannot be racist because they do not have power.

However, this shield blocks Blacks and other people of color holding a position of power from carrying out antiracist work since they do not seem to have any kind of power and White people have the entire power. This underlines that people of color do not have the power required to refute racist policies and eliminate racial inequities in their own domains of influence, the areas where they have power to give rise to change. This powerless defense further blocks people of color from charges of racism even when they are regenerating racist policies and justifying them with similar racist ideas to the White people they term racist. This defense further

44

makes people of color insensitive to the idea of capitalizing on their limited power to coerce people of color for their own advantage.

The powerless defense follows the example of all other racist ideas, overestimates White people and underestimates Black people. It takes away all power from Black managers and policymakers.

White power controls the United States but not completely. Blacks do have some degree of power in different roles. It renders the "powerless defense" argument invalid and makes it possible for Blacks to indulge in racism.

Chapter 12: Class

Class Racist

Such a racist engages in the racialization of the classes, endorsing policies of racial capitalism against race-classes, and justifying them by racist ideas regarding those race-classes.

Antiracist Anticapitalist

This term refers to a person who competes against racial capitalism.

Race-classes

This term refers to the racial groups that are at the intersection of race and class. Poor people are a class. Black people are a race. Black poor people are a race-class. When we call poor people lazy, we are voicing an elitist idea. When we call Black people lazy, we are demonstrating a racist idea. When we claim that Black poor people are lazier than poor Whites, White elites and Black elites, we are talking at the intersection of racist and elitist ideas. This is a conceptual intersection that develops class racism.

When a policy exploits poor people, it means it is an elitist policy. When a policy exploits Black people, it means it is a racist policy. When a policy exploits Black poor people, it does so at the meeting of racist and elitist policies, a policy joint of class racism. When we racialize classes, endorse racist policies against those race-classes and justify them by racist ideas, we are taking part in class racism.

Class racism is common in both Whites and Blacks. Whites chastise poor Whites as "White trash." Racist Blacks degrade poor Blacks as 'them niggers' who dwell in the ghetto. Constructs made of "White trash" and "ghetto Blacks" are the most apparent ideological types of class racism.

To be antiracist means leveling the race-classes. It also means considering policies instead of people to be responsible for the economic disparities between the equal race-classes.

A lot of people, especially capitalists, define capitalism to be markets, market rules, competition and advantages of winning. By doing this, they isolate capitalism from racism, imperialism, sexism and stealing. History does not corroborate this particular definition of capitalism. All the above-mentioned things engulfed by capitalism have been there for a long time before the ascent of capitalism in the modern world. Capitalism brought racially irregular playing fields, international theft, unidirectional affluence that surges skyward infinitely to this blend. Markets have not been even playing fields since the rise of racial capitalism. Working people have not been able to contest equally with capitalists. Black people have not been able to compete equally with White people. African countries have not been able to compete equally with European countries. Rules have favored the wealthy and White countries. Humanity requests honest definitions of capitalism and racism rooted in the true existing history of these conjoined twins.

Loving capitalism translates into loving racism. Loving racism leads to loving capitalism. A single vicious body shows these conjoined twins as its two sides. The notion that capitalism is just about free trade, competition, free markets, supply and demand, and private ownership of the means of production working for a profit is ridiculous. Capitalism is fundamentally racist and racism is fundamentally capitalist. Identical 'unnatural causes' spawned both capitalism and racism. They will expire together from 'unnatural causes' someday. Or racial capitalism will continue to persist and steal and lead to inequities if activists keep battling the conjoined twins separately.

Chapter 13: Space

Space Racism

It refers to an influential collection of racist policies that give birth to inequity in resources between racialized spaces or strive to remove particular racialized spaces, which is validated by racist ideas regarding racialized spaces.

Space Antiracism

It refers to a powerful collection of antiracist policies that create equity between integrated and sheltered racialized spaces, which is validated by antiracist ideas regarding racialized spaces.

Kendi called his African American studies space a Black space since it was chiefly governed by Black bodies, Black cultures, Black thoughts and Black histories. The spaces at Temple University governed principally by White bodies, White cultures, White thoughts and White histories were not underlined to be White.

They concealed the widespread Whiteness in their spaces under the blanket of color blindness.

Racist Americans are guilty of denouncing Black neighborhoods as places defined by homicides and deadly violence but do not follow the same pattern when it comes to White neighborhoods and fail to link these to the disparate number of White males who carry out mass shootings. They do not notice the day-to-day violence that happens on highways that mostly take White suburbanites to their homes.

Racist power racializes both people and space; the ghetto, the interior city, the third world. A space becomes racialized when a racial group is recognized to either govern the space or contribute to the obvious majority in the space. For example, a Black space is usually either managed by Black people or a space where Black people have the majority. Policies of space racism provide excessive resources to White spaces and offer scarce resources to non-White spaces.

Ideas of space racism justify inequity between resources by mapping out a racial hierarchy of space, putting White spaces on a pedestal and making them seem like heaven while demoting non-White spaces and making them seem like hell.

Resources define a space. However, the conjoined twins of capitalism and racism divide up resources. Weighing spaces across race-classes against one another is completely unfair. We need to compare poor Black neighborhoods to similarly poor White neighborhoods, instead of substantially wealthier White neighborhoods. We need to compare small Black businesses to equally small White businesses instead of rich White corporations.

Americans have witnessed the rational end of segregationist strategy, moving from slavery to Jim Crow to mass incarceration to border walls. The logical conclusion of antiracist strategy is equal and open access to public housings, open access to every integrated White space, integrated Black space, integrated Native space, integrated Middle Eastern space, integrated Asian space, integrated Latinx space, which are as equally resourced as culturally distinct. This category of spaces affixes economic, cultural and political power. Examples include a newspaper editorial board, a school board or a House of Representatives. In such spaces, none of the races prevails and joint antiracist power prevails. This makes a statement about diversity, which integrationists only consider to be worthy on paper.

Antiracist strategy counters desegregation with a type of integration and racial solidarity. Desegregation refers to the eradication of all hurdles to every racialized space. To be antiracist means endorsing the deliberate integration of bodies drawn by cultural difference, a collective humanity. Integration means resources instead of bodies. Being antiracist means campaigning for resource equity by questioning the racist policies that lead to resource inequity. Racial solidarity means clearly recognizing, endorsing, and shielding integrated racial spaces. Being antiracist means linking and fostering difference among racial groups.

However, antiracist strategy surpasses the integrationist notion that asserts that Black spaces cannot be equal to White spaces, that thinks that Black spaces have a negative impact on Black people.

Chapter 14: Gender

Gender Racism

It refers to a potent assortment of racist policies that give rise to inequity between race-genders and are validated by racist ideas about race-genders.

Gender Antiracism

It refers to a powerful array of antiracist policies that give birth to equity between race-genders and are authenticated by antiracist ideas about race-genders.

Kendi's parents, along with millions of other people, questioned the multiplying percentage of Black children being born to single mothers in the 1970s and 1980s. People questioned the sexuality of young Black mothers. The panic also resulted from some flawed ideas including the existence of two bad parents being better than just one good one, the attendance of an abusive Black father being better for a child than his absence, and so on.

Before the midterm elections in 1994, political scientist Charles Murray ensured Americans were aware of the percentage of Black children born into single-parent homes. Murray put the blame on the welfare system. Kendi's parents and other liberals blamed sexual recklessness, pathologizing poverty, a disgraceful disregard for the prospects stemming from 1960s activism and a detachment from the premarital abstinence of Christ. They were quite wrong because the growing percentage of Black children being born into single-parent households was not because of single Black mothers having a higher number of children but because of married Black women having a lesser number of children. Kendi's parents and a huge number of other Americans were detached from racial reality and were quick to demonize this category of single mothers. Only Black feminists defended them. However, Kendi's mother did have a feminist stance on a number of matters.

Racist and sexist power differentiates between race-genders, racial or gender groups at the crossing of race and gender. Black people make a race. Women make a gender. By categorizing Black women, we classify a race-gender. A sexist policy generates inequities between men and women. A racist policy generates inequities between racial groups. When a policy generates inequities between race-genders, it is gendered racism or gender racism.

To be antiracist means refuting the hierarchy of both races and race-genders. To be feminist means rebuffing the hierarchy of both genders and race-genders. To be really antiracist means to be feminist as well. To be really feminist means to be antiracist as well. To be antiracist and feminist equals balancing the different race-genders and basing the inequities between the equal race-genders in the policies of gender racism.

Gender racism was the culprit behind the increasing percentage of involuntary sterilizations of Black women by eugenicist physicians. It led to two hundred thousand cases in 1970 and seven hundred thousand in 1980. Gender racism plays a role in Black women with some collegiate education earning less than White women with just high school degrees and Black women being required to have higher level degrees before they can make more money than White women with just high school degrees. Black women and Native women suffer from poverty at a greater rate than any other race-gender group. Latinx and Black women make the least amount of money, while Asian and White men make the most.

Black women are three to four times more likely to lose their lives to pregnancy - related causes than are White women. Black women with a higher degree are more likely to lose their babies than White women with a less than 8th grade education. The chances of Black women to be imprisoned are double those of White women.

Gender racism affects men of color and White women too, regardless of whether they acknowledge it. White women's opposition to Black feminism and intersectional theory has been self-destructive, stopping resisters from comprehending their own subjugation. The intersection of sexism and racism represses White women in some cases. An example is as follows: Sexist ideas of "real women" as "weak" and racist beliefs about White women as the idealized woman cross to generate the gender-racist notion that the apex of womanhood is the weak White woman. This gender racism made millions of White men and women abhor the strong White woman running for president in 2016 i. e. Hilary Clinton. Black women are portrayed as characterless and hypersexual to portray white women as virtuous and asexual to control the latter's sexuality.

Male opposition to Black feminism has been equally self-destructive, stopping resistors from comprehending their own subjugation. The intersection of sexism and racism ends up oppressing men of color in some cases. Black men end up reinforcing repressive tropes by reinforcing specific sexist notions. An example tells us that 'racist ideas' of Black men as not actually men and sexist notions of 'real men' as strong crisscross to spawn the gender racism of the weak Black man, lesser than the summit of "manhood, which is the strong White man.

Chapter 15: Sexuality

Queer Racism

It refers to a powerful collection of racist policies that give rise to inequity between race-sexualities and are validated by racist notions regarding race-sexualities.

Queer Antiracism

It refers to a commanding assembly of antiracist policies that create equity between race–sexualities and are validated by antiracist notions about race-sexualities.

Racist and homophobic power makes a distinction between race-sexualities, racial (or sexuality) groups at the crossing of race and sexuality. Latinx people make a race. Homosexuals fall into the category of a sexuality. Latinx homosexuals make a race-sexuality. A homophobic policy generates inequities between heterosexuals and homosexuals. A racist policy generates inequities between racial groups. Queer racism generates inequities between race-sexualities. It generates circumstances where 32% of children being raised by Black male same-sex couples dwell in poverty, compared to 14% of children being raised by White male same-sex couples, 13% of children being raised by Black heterosexuals, and 7% of children being raised by White heterosexuals. The racial inequality is almost equally pronounced for children being raised by female same-sex couples. The children of Black queer couples are more plausible to dwell in poverty since their parents are more probably poor than White queer and Black heterosexual couples.

Homophobia cannot be isolated from racism. They have interconnected for a long time. Queer antiracism considers all the race-sexualities to be equal, attempting to eradicate the inequities between the race-sexualities. We cannot claim to be antiracist if we are transphobic or homophobic. We should keep asserting that 'all Black lives matter.' All Black lives include the lives of poor transgender Black women, possibly the most oppressed and violated of all the Black intersectional groups.

Chapter 16: Failure

Activist

An activist is someone who has a history of power or policy change.

Racism persists because we have failed to develop racist societies. Antiracist solutions and strategies have failed. Fear stops us from being antiracist. We need to be daring to be antiracist. Courage means being strong enough to do the right thing while encountering fear. Antiracist ideas will let us know what right is. If you try, you can gain strength from fear. Be afraid of what will happen if you fail to resist. Be afraid of weakness. Work to achieve this so that everybody can have more than what they presently have.

Chapter 17: Success

We are afraid of success. Success means the predomination of antiracist power and policy. Success translates into equal opportunities and thus results between the equal groups. It means people blaming policies instead of people for societal issues. It means racist power dwelling on the boundaries, like antiracist power presently does. It means antiracist ideas are part of common sense, like racist ideas are today.

Success and failure are not set in stone. What steps we are ready to take will shape our generation's take. We need to ask ourselves whether we are ready to tolerate the exhausting fight against racist power and policy. Are we ready to change the antiracist power we collect within us to antiracist power in our society?

Chapter 18: Survival

Racism is all around us in advanced stages. It has gripped the United States like cancer. Kendi had cancer and survived, where his wife Sadiqa was with him every step of the way. We can survive racism by treating it like cancer. We can treat racism by linking the treatment plans in different areas. However, we first need to believe that we can fight and get rid of it.

Conclusion

Kendi teaches us to fight racism the following way:

How to be an Antiracist in Consecutive Steps

1. Stop using the 'I am not a racist' or 'I can't be racist' shield of denial

2. Admit the definition of racist (someone who is endorsing racist policies or demonstrating racist ideas)

3. Admit the racist policies you support and racist notions you express.

4. Accept their source.

5. Recognize the definition of antiracist

6. Battle for antiracist power and policy in your spaces.

7. Stay at the antiracist intersection where racism is blended with other biases.

8. Think with antiracist ideas.

Check out other summaries

1. Summary of **_Robin DiAngelo's White Fragility: Why It's So Hard for White People to Talk About Racism_**
Link: https://www.amazon.com/dp/B08C4BGLHP

2. Summary of **_Brené Brown's Daring Greatly:_** How the Courage to Be Vulnerable Transforms the Way We Live, Love, Parent, and Lead
Link: https://www.amazon.com/dp/B08BLPD1DW

3. Summary of **_The Power of Habit - Charles Duhigg_**
This summary is for everyone. It tells us that our life is a direct result of our habits. We can change our life by changing our habits. Even if we start with just one thing, it can leave a powerful impact on the other areas of our life as well. We have the reins of our destiny by improving our ways. The summary offers a detailed yet concise version of the core lessons of the book. You can benefit immensely from it.

Link: https://www.amazon.com/dp/B07YTJ6WM7

4. Summary of *Just Mercy - Bryan Stevenson*

This summary captures the attention of its readers and holds it. It includes all important details of the main arc of the book. It also makes the problems with America's justice system absolutely clear. It pulls on our heartstrings by sharing the plight of several victims of the very system that is supposed to protect them. It opens our eyes and motivates us to do something to make things right for others. In sum, this summary is both inspirational and multidimensional.

Link: https://www.amazon.com/dp/B07XRTVW63

5. Summary of *The Magic of Thinking Big - David J. Schwartz*

This is an extremely high quality summary of the book, which takes into account every single piece of useful insight. It makes everything concise and easy to remember. This book will change your life in a short span of time.

Link: https://www.amazon.com/dp/B07WZRJTH6

6. Summary of *The Power of Now - Eckhart Tolle*

The Power of Now is not like any other book. It will teach you a new way of life. You might think that you have no other presence than your mind and physical body but you do not know your true self. The Power of Now will help you be present and live in the current moment like never before. It will liberate you from the noise of your mind and help you achieve inner peace. You will truly learn to live and connect with the Divine after reading and understanding this book.

Link: https://www.amazon.com/dp/B002361MLA

7. Summary of *The Complete Guide to Fasting – Dr. Jason Fung*

This summary of Life in the Fasting Lane is a refreshing version of the book. It keeps its readers informed so that they can make wise decisions about their diet and life. It presents its points such that its readers can understand and make the most of fasting to improve their lives. It makes fasting simpler and offers the background and practical aspects of the original in the best possible manner.

Link: https://www.amazon.com/dp/B082VG8Y9Q

8. Summary of *Life in the Fasting Lane – Dr. Jason Fung*

This summary of Life in the Fasting Lane is a refreshing version of the book. It keeps its readers informed so that they can make wise decisions about their diet and life. It presents its points such that its readers can understand and make the most of fasting to improve their lives. It makes fasting simpler and offers the background and practical aspects of the original in the best possible manner.

Link: https://www.amazon.com/dp/B088KNRPKP

Made in the USA
Middletown, DE
15 July 2020

12708107R00043